Aa

A was an apple pie

An English Nursery Rhyme

illustrated by

Etienne Delessert

Creative Editions

MANKATO, MINNESOTA

Aa

A was an apple pie

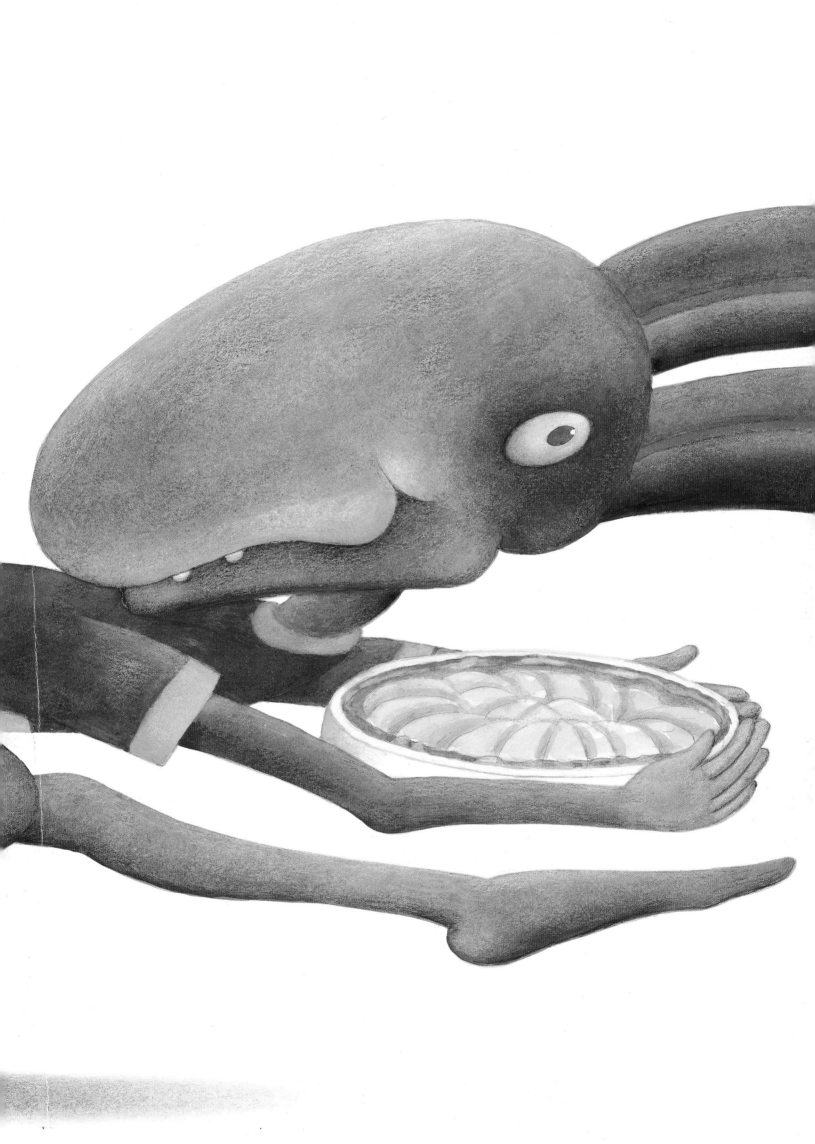

Bb

B bit it

Cc

C cut it

Dd

D dealt it

Ee

E ate it

Ff

F fought for it

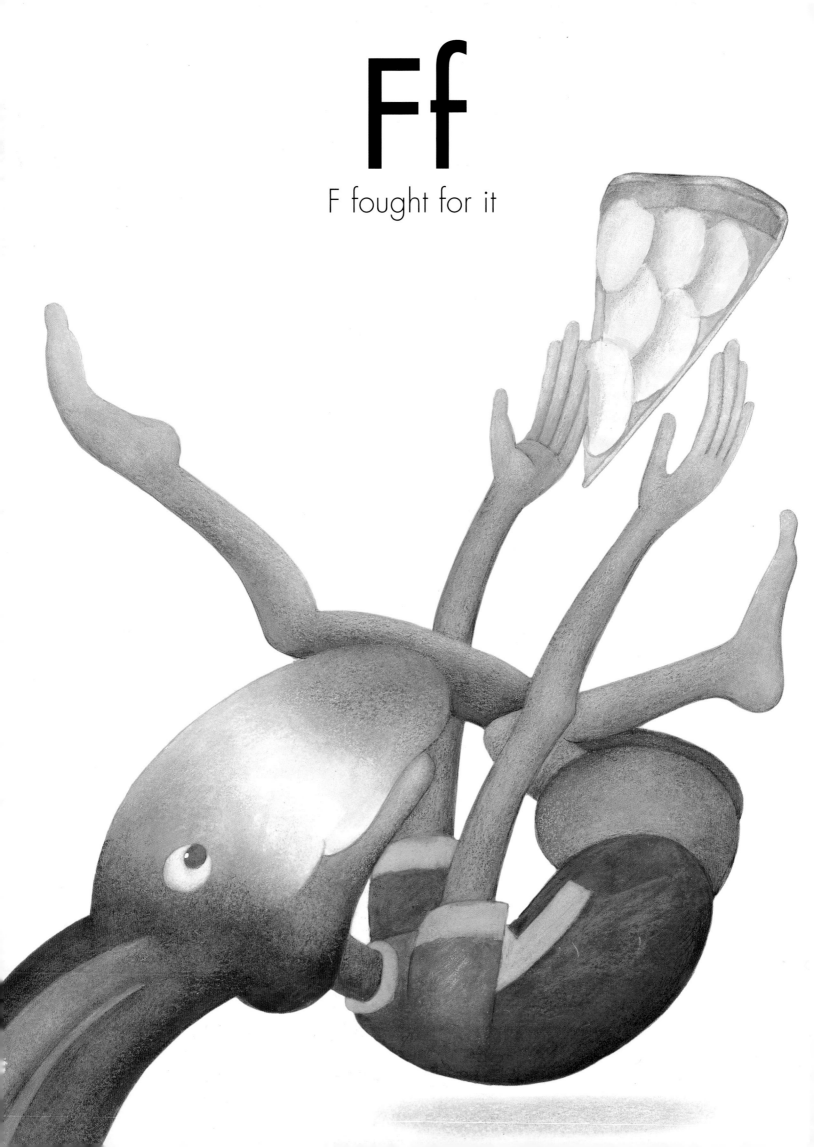

Gg

G got it

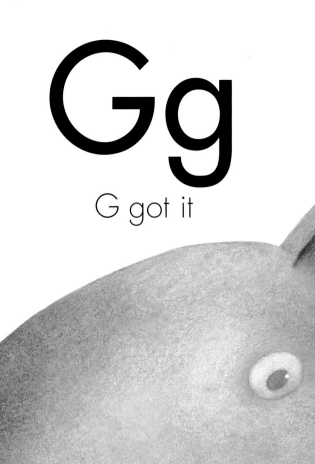

Hh

H had it

Ii

I inspected it

Jj

J jumped for it

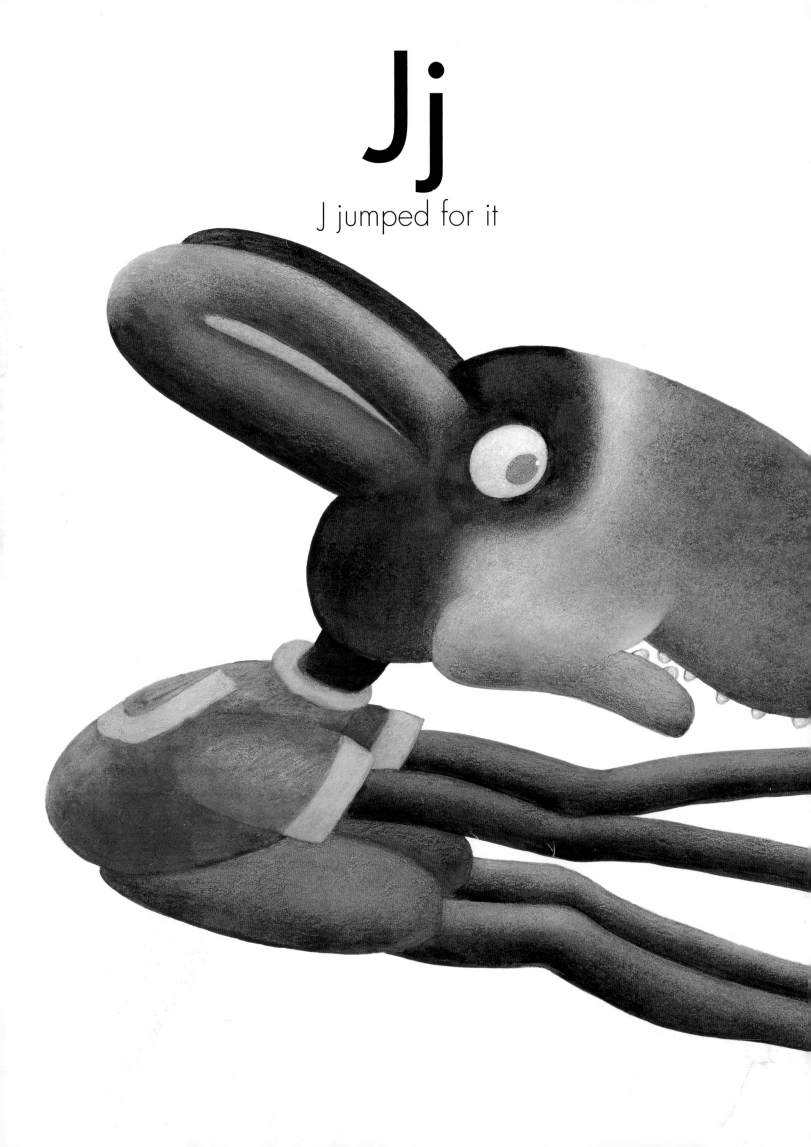

Kk

K kept it

Ll

L longed for it

Mm

M mourned for it

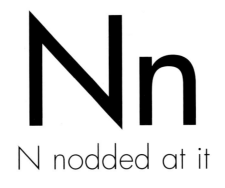

Nn

N nodded at it

Oo

O opened it

Pp

P peeped in it

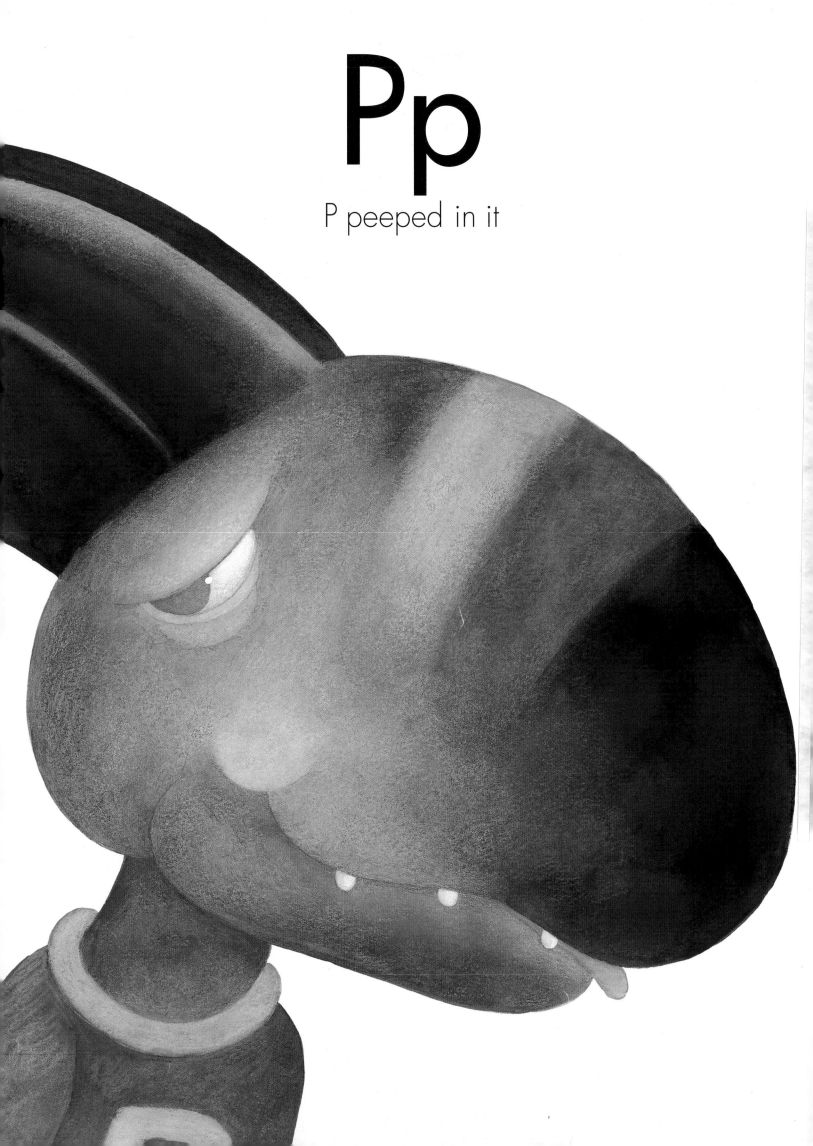

Qq

Q quartered it

Rr

R ran for it

Ss

S stole it

Tt

T took it

Uu

U upset it

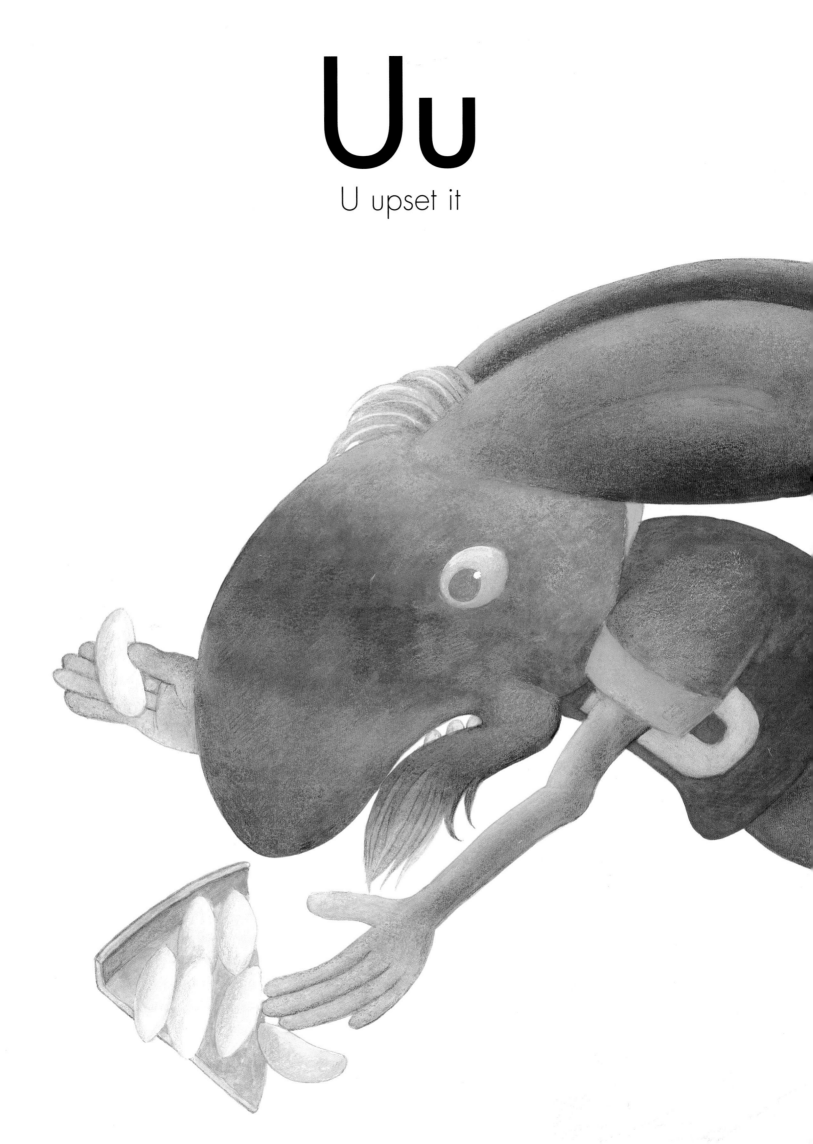

Vv

V viewed it

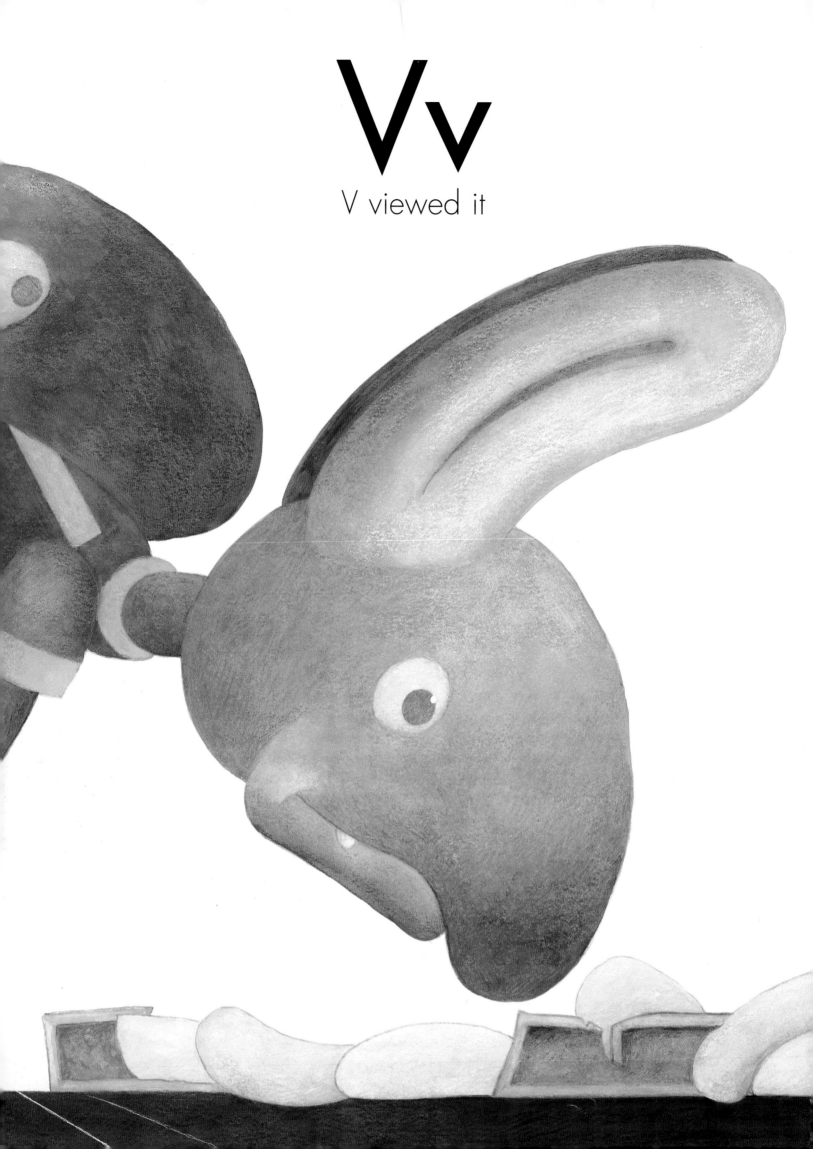

Ww

W wanted it

Xx Yy Zz

X, Y, Z, and ampersand
All wished for a piece in hand.

Published in 2005 by Creative Editions

123 South Broad Street, Mankato, MN 56001 USA

Creative Editions is an imprint of The Creative Company.

Designed by Rita Marshall
Printed in Italy

Library of Congress Cataloging-in-Publication Data

Delessert, Etienne.

A was an apple pie / [illustrated by] Etienne Delessert.

ISBN 1-56846-196-8

1. English language—Alphabet—Juvenile literature. I. Title.

PE1155.D445 2005

428.1—dc22   2004061174

First Edition 5 4 3 2 1